Its All In The Price

Its All In The Price

A Business Solution to the Economy

PETER WILLIAM BAILEY

Copyright © 2012 by Peter William Bailey.

ISBN: Softcover   978-1-4771-2698-1
          Ebook   978-1-4771-2699-8

All rights reserved. No part of this book may be reproduced or transmitted in any form or by any means, electronic or mechanical, including photocopying, recording, or by any information storage and retrieval system, without permission in writing from the copyright owner.

This book was printed in the United States of America.

To order additional copies of this book, contact:
Xlibris Corporation
0-800-644-6988
www.xlibrispublishing.co.uk
Orders@xlibrispublishing.co.uk

CONTENTS

Foreword	The economists and politicians mainly have it wrong	7
Chapter 1	Defining an Economy	9
Chapter 2	Maximum Economic Efficiency	12
Chapter 3	Basics	15
Chapter 4	Control Is in the Hands of the Government	17
Chapter 5	Taxes and Taxation	20
Chapter 6	Inflation	32
Chapter 7	Running a Country	36
Chapter 8	Ministry of Business	45
Chapter 9	What Could Happen If We Do Not Change?	47
Chapter 10	Trade and Balance of Payments	49
Chapter 11	Comment on the World at Large	50
Chapter 12	Politics	53
Chapter 13	The Possible Future of the Green Theme	56

FOREWORD

The economists and politicians mainly have it wrong

No country in the world today appears to be well run, but then I don't know about all the countries. Most seem to have economic problems of one kind or another, one of the biggest being unemployment. Advents over the years and present-day practices show me that no one seems to know fully what economy is about and, therefore, cannot run a country effectively.

From any number of the policies being followed, political beliefs and economic theories. this is not surprising.

Statements like belt-tightening and hardship to pull an economy round show a lack of understanding. It sounds correct, but the opposite position is far more logical and true. The economy will expand in boom conditions and not in recession.

The ability to pull out of times of recession is easy if you know how—very difficult otherwise—because the way out is the opposite way to which people believe they should go.

The hiking of interest rates by the governor of the central bank to fight inflation, induced by government tax increases, illustrates how wrong we have been. The opposite position is more often the correct one. The central bank should not interfere in the control of the economy anyway. The Ministry of Finance should be in control because only they control all the factors.

The tax systems, and particularly income tax, show how wrong they have been. When it can be appreciated that all tax is paid by the community from net pay at the till point, then, and only then, can we appreciate how bad income tax and other taxes are in the context of the economy.

The British Conservative Party's belief that wealth trickles down to the poor is another opposite, and wealth flows *up* from the poor.

There is a fairly general acceptance that poverty and unemployment are a fact of life and here to stay. Nothing could be further from the truth. Maximum economic efficiency requires full employment.

The main problem is that whilst thousands of people have undergone training in economics and political science, there is still something missing, and hopefully, this is it. The earlier teachings were somewhat blinkered, applied to a different set of circumstances, and failed to recognise the alternative and often the opposite viewpoint.

An economy can and does operate only one way.

CHAPTER 1

The first part analyses and puts into perspective what should be involved in the running of a country. It requires that we understand what an economy is about and what it should achieve.

Defining an Economy

My definition is as follows:

A community of people working to supply their own needs and wants, who may be organised by leaders and entrepreneurs into organisations and companies with tools and equipment to boost their productive capacity.

The validity of this definition is that if we take a community of people stranded in isolation anywhere in the world, it will first need to appoint a leadership to make the rules and regulations by which they will live. The leadership then has two choices: to follow the past, when skills and knowledge were limited and to allow the people to eke out their own living from the land to the best of their abilities. Or in a more enlightened way, to organise the people and the skills to produce what they require in a more efficient and productive manner. As skills improve, machinery, equipment, and methods develop, so more can be produced or a greater variety of goods and services provided—all or those that improve the standard of living and the quality of life.

The definition to some extent was recognised in the communist theory in a few short words—'From each according to his ability, to each according to his needs'.

The people of the community are producing goods and services for their own needs and wants to improve their standard of living and quality of life. The people who are producing are the end consumers. People are needed to produce, and the same people are needed to consume what is produced. Government and business organisations combine the efforts of people to improve productivity. Money would not be an essential commodity in production, and the object of increasing productivity would be to improve the standard of living of the community.

Most countries developed from a number of small communities (tribes) with leaders to a countrywide single leadership, usually a monarch, who amassed and distributed wealth to a favoured few. The majority of people started at peasant level.

Because Karl Marx recognised that there would be problems with any monetary system because it allowed some people to amass wealth, he advocated a cashless society. However, this could not work. A monetary system was required to provide the community with freedom of choice and a method of control in the distribution of the goods and services produced.

Money

With the introduction of money, the definition changes, but the basics remain:

A community of people working to supply their own needs and wants, organised by leaders and entrepreneurs into organisations and companies with tools and equipment to boost their productive capacity. Monetary systems provide payment to the workers that allow them to convert the result of their efforts into their personal requirements. The leadership will impose taxes and levies on the community to pay for its own expense and provide community services where necessary.

Money not only provides workers with a choice of goods, it controls the distribution in proportion to their efforts (income). It also means that the government, instead of collecting goods and services from the people to maintain itself, can impose taxes in a monetary form. Money provides entrepreneurs and business leaders, who organise the community with the ability to expand, freedom to choose what they produce, the price that the community has to pay within economic limitations, and the people that they employ. Profit becomes the motivating factor of the entrepreneur, and the limitations are provided by competition.

The definition includes the provision of community services by the government. This is a necessary function of the government to provide orderly development. People must be educated and have access to health facilities. Roads and other means of communication have to be provided. The government has to ensure that all the basic requirements are developed either through taxation or through private enterprise. The prime concern of government should be the welfare of the people and the development of the community as a whole. As we will see, this will lead to the most successful economy all around.

CHAPTER 2

Maximum Economic Efficiency

Maximum economic efficiency can be achieved only through maximum employment, the most efficient and effective organisation, and production methods, together with balanced production and consumption.

In a cashless society, no thought would be given to unemployment. Everyone would be expected to do their bit and directed to work for the benefit of the community as a whole. The more people working, the less the individual effort has to be and the higher the standard of living that will be attained. It is the proof that everyone must work with as much efficiency as possible. The monetary economy should, and can, have the same objectives in mind.

There is little point in producing goods and services that cannot be absorbed by the community. The spending power of the community must be sufficient to buy the goods and services produced. There will always be a cushion effect produced by increasing or decreasing stock levels.

Excess goods produced may be exported, but to balance the books, an equal amount of goods should be imported. The spending power of the community must, therefore, be sufficient to absorb the goods and services that are also imported.

This balance between production and payment to workers is vital, not for social or any other reason other than to provide a sound, balanced marketplace. Common sense should reveal that it is not possible to have the productive units in one country and non-working consumers in another.

Businesses require only a good marketplace in order to operate successfully.

Employment and Unemployment

Visualise a community of people developing without a monetary system. Everyone would be expected to work. It starts with everyone fending for themselves, hunters and gatherers, building their own huts and feeding themselves and their families. Introduce the chief who wants to develop the community by developing skilled people through a division of labour. Then we have builders in the building industry, people in the clothing industry, and people in the food industry all with tools and equipment to help them. The system can be developed and efficiency improved, but it should be noted that all would have to contribute by working. People would not be allowed not to work and still enjoy the benefits. It is a fact that the harder the people work, the more they will produce and the better off they will be. As production increases, the chief will develop other industries and recreation activities. He could not have people idle. As communities grow, there is the need to improve the infrastructure, the need to make a greater variety of goods, and the need for new thought processes. It is to note that money is required in the system to provide for freedom of choice and the ability of business to expand through the creation of wealth.

There is no reason why in the modern world we should tolerate unemployment and accept that some people will be unemployed. It costs money for people to be unemployed because the government cannot be responsible for people dying of starvation because they have no work.

It is vital that Western governments change. They need to get their countries on to a more competitive basis and stop accepting that goods can be made cheaper elsewhere. The world will be a sorry place if the markets disappear, and it must be recognised that as the Asian markets develop their internal economies, they will become less reliant on the West for business, and as the Western countries unemployment grows, the taxes will increase, the investment will become less, and they will become poor.

Basics

One needs to appreciate that there was, and is, only man and natural resources in the world. The product of people's efforts creates all the rest whether it is buildings, machinery, motor vehicles, or wealth. The world as we know it started with nothing. Communities developed, and the leaderships of these communities were usually responsible for the rate of development. Maximum economic efficiency comes with maximum employment and effort.

CHAPTER 3

Basics

There are only man and natural resources in the economy. Only people have and control money, whilst natural resources are, or were, free. People have created the countries and economies we live in, with all their faults and problems. People have built the buildings, made the roads, and made the tools and equipment—all things required to improve productive capacity and the standard of living.

The origins of mankind show that there were only man and natural resources in the beginning. All development has been achieved by man, utilising the natural resources available. Buildings, plant and machinery, motor cars, roads, aircraft, food, clothing, and so on are all the products of man from the resources available. Natural resources start out free with primary industries, be it land on which we grow crops, mine for minerals, and fish any sea products or products from the air. There is cost added in respect of labour and machinery, and the products are then passed directly to consumers or the next production process at a price to cover the costs involved and a return to the entrepreneur. There may be a number of processes in the manufacture of products, but the end result of all business and manufacture is a product sold to a consumer, who is a part of a community.

Business may consume raw materials and other products and may sell its production to another business, but business is not an end consumer; its costs are built in to the products or services that it sells; only people can be, and are, end consumers of products and services. This fits in with the definition that people work to provide goods and services for themselves. It has to be remembered that business and government exist only to provide goods and services to the people of the community.

Although land was free in the beginning, over time, man has often alienated this resource, and it has thereby attained a value. No attempt has yet been made to capitalise on the sea and the air. The cost of land or its rent, derived from the value of money and the normal economic laws of supply and demand, has, therefore, to be taken into the cost of production and distribution.

CHAPTER 4

Control Is in the Hands of the Government

The economy can be controlled and driven in any given direction. It is the leadership or the government that makes the decisions that control the economy.

The business cycle has an explanation.

The economy does behave in a specific manner.

The government makes the decisions that control the economy. Problems can arise when there are different levels for government in making decisions on taxes such as local councils and mainstream government. If they are not coordinated there will be problems.

The economy is, by definition, about the *productivity* and the *spending power* of the community. Whilst many believe that it is about finance, it is difficult, but not impossible, to run an economy without money.

If spending power diminishes, then the demand for goods goes down, which in turn reduces the number of people needed to produce goods. If spending power goes up, then there will be a demand for more goods, which will result in greater production and more people being employed. In a cashless society, the demand for goods and services will usually far exceed production because there is not the controlling factor of income to restrict purchasing to productive output.

Demand changes constantly for a variety of reasons. The demand for some products will decrease, whilst the demand for others will increase over time, and there will be a constant demand for innovation. Modern manufacturing processes are quite mechanised and require fewer and fewer people in manufacturing processes but need more in research and development. Recreation, travel, and sports are all service industries that can and will develop as overall spending power improves.

All changes in the fortunes of a country revolve around and are explainable through changes in the spending power of the community. There are constantly changing conditions. The Internet has made a huge difference to the way in which people buy.

Government policies can change the effective spending power in the community—things like free, or paying, health and education services, tax and/or interest rate changes, and property rent versus ownership. Accommodation can cause major changes and can absorb a disproportionate share of incomes.

Innovation, efficiencies in the methods of production, changes in the goods and services on offer, and the quality of life of the average person contribute to the change process.

Change can cause an upturn or downturn in the spending power available, and the constantly improving standard of living through invention presents its own problems.

Business Cycle

The business cycle is very much about spending power. In an upward cycle, community spending power starts to increase; the improvement is reflected in business returns, and business will require more people. The number of people employed grows, and the rewards to employees improve, creating more spending power in the economy. This situation can compound itself until there are boom conditions. Inflation sets in where demand begins to outstrip supply, and the government steps in to curb spending power.

Property prices and rentals are liable to increase disproportionately under these conditions.

In a downward cycle, consumer spending power reduces for whatever reason and business returns at retail level decline. Demands on manufacturers also decline with a consequent reduction in the number of people employed and restrictions on increments and rewards to the people. This position will compound itself into a recession and, if not turned around, into a depression.

Trades union demands and normal pay increments to employees help to alleviate these circumstances. However, trades unions are at their weakest during a recession and high unemployment, and employers are reluctant to give wage increments.

The quick solution to a recession is to increase spending power, that is, reduce taxes or increase wages—a difficult position to accept when the economy and business is not doing well and the government is short of finances. However, the change can be very quick.

Large government expenditure to 'kick start' an economy reflects this position but is unpredictable and may not work in some circumstances. It is far easier and more effective to push wages and salaries up by say 2.5 per cent.

As mentioned earlier, spending power changes with annual increments to employees, changes in inflation rates, changes in interest rates, and changes in taxation. There are many causes for change.

CHAPTER 5

Taxes and Taxation

The economy is largely about spending power, and most of the confusion and lack of control has arisen from the tax systems that have been developed over the years.

The community actually pays the full taxes from net income. The true point of collection for all taxes is the till point, and the true taxpayer is the consumer, irrespective of what people have been led to believe and what pay advices to workers might show.

Economic efficiency is at its best where the income to spending power ratio is 100 per cent. That is to say that income converts wholly into spending power.

The best and most efficient form of taxation is a single graduated VAT system.

Income tax is probably the worst means of collecting tax and should be scrapped with most of the other means of collecting taxes. Free market conditions dictate that there should be just a single system of VAT taxation.

There are large amounts of tax collected so that the government can pay taxes to itself. Both the government and the private business sector exist to provide goods and services to the general community, and their prices and costs are very often considerably inflated by taxes. It is possible to reduce the whole cost structure of government and business by removing the unnecessary taxes.

Whilst the acceptability of tax changes by the community is given every consideration, the economic implications of tax changes are very often given little consideration, and it is essential to put these things into perspective. The winning formula will be where employment costs are the lowest and spending power the highest.

Income Tax

Everyone has been led to believe that this is a just and fair system of taxation so that everyone contributes to the tax burden. The virtues of the system providing for differentials between married and single persons and persons with children are or have been mentioned. It is also believed to narrow the so-called wage gap.

A total misconception of the truth. *Income tax is a tax on employment.* It adds to the cost of employment, and with incomes based on gross income, it actually widens the wage gap.

It is a tax that is actually paid twice. It is a deduction from income, which is what we see every time we receive a wage packet. What we do not see, and what is not appreciated, is that we do, in fact, pay almost all taxes, which include income taxes in the price of the goods and services that we buy.

The best way to explain this is to freeze income tax and for the employer to pay the tax of its employees as an employment tax, reducing the employees' gross income to net income. The employee is no worse off; he still gets his net pay, which does not change, and the employer is no worse off because his cost of employment is the same. The price of the goods and services do not change because the costs have not changed. The government is no worse off because it is still receiving the tax.

It can now be appreciated that the tax is still being paid, and the employee as a consumer is still paying the tax. The tax is included in the cost of the goods and services that he buys, which all goes to show that, as income tax, he was paying the tax twice.

The consumer actually pays the entire tax burden from his net income. Business is but a conduit, through which the taxes are routed to the consumer. All taxes charged to business add to the cost of the business and raise the price charged to the consumer.

Only when we can fully appreciate this fact, can we appreciate that income tax as such can and should be discontinued. A better demonstration is given below:

When, Where, and How Tax Is Paid

Because the income tax or PAYE system has been in operation for so long and is ingrained in our system of taxation, we believe that we pay our tax when we earn our income.

I have to be insane to try to tell people who have a payslip each week or month, telling them how much income tax they have paid that they do not actually pay that tax and that they actually pay their taxes at another place and point in time.

This is how it works, the figures are imaginary, and for demonstration alone, they could represent any currency and any value:

ITS ALL IN THE PRICE

Present Position

EMPLOYER CONTRIBUTION TO NAT INS	100
GROSS PAY OF EMPLOYEES	1000
LESS	
INCOME TAX	-200
NATIONAL INSURANCE	-100
PENSION	
NET PAY	700

COMPANY COSTS

GROSS PAY ABOVE PLUS PAY OVERHEAD	1100
OTHER PRODUCTION COSTS	2000
OVERHEADS	500
LOCAL AND ANY OTHER TAXES	50
COST	3650
PROFIT AFTER TAX	25
TAX	5
SELLING PRICE	3680
VAT	552
TOTAL SELLING PRICE	4232

The fact of the matter is that the employer has to pay the employee more money for him to pay his taxes and other deductions.

So we change it, we leave the employee with his net pay and make the deductions a cost to the employer.

The cost to the employer is the same, the pay to the employee is the same and the price at the end is the same, Nothing changes except the wording and consolidation of now duplicate expenses. Here it is:

EMPLOYER CONTRIBUTION TO NAT INS ETC

GROSS PAY OF EMPLOYEES

EMPLOYMENT TAX	200
NATIONAL INSURANCE	200
PENSION	
NET PAY	700

COMPANY COSTS

GROSS PAY ABOVE PLUS PAY OVERHEAD	1100
OTHER PRODUCTION COSTS	2000
OVERHEADS	500
LOCAL AND ANY OTHER TAXES	50
COST	3650
PROFIT AFTER TAX	25
TAX	5
SELLING PRICE	3680
VAT	552
TOTAL SELLING PRICE	4232

At this point we can now re allocate the taxes paid by the employer. It will not affect the employee, his pay stays the same, and the end price to the consumer will stay the same.

ITS ALL IN THE PRICE

```
   EMPLOYER CONTRIBUTION TO NAT INS
 ETC

 GROSS PAY OF EMPLOYEES


 EMPLOYMENT TAX
 NATIONAL INSURANCEPENSION

 NET PAY                                        700
```

COMPANY COSTS

GROSS AND NET PAY OF EMPLOYEES	700
OTHER PRODUCTION COSTS	2000
OVERHEADS	500
LOCAL AND ANY OTHER TAXES	0
COST	3200
PROFIT AFTER TAX	25
TAX	0
SELLING PRICE	3225
VAT	552
ADD	
EMPLOYMENT TAX 200	
NATIONAL INSURANCE 200	
LOCAL AND OTHER TAXES 50	
TAX ON PROFIT 5	455
TOTAL SELLING PRICE	4232

I have moved all the company taxes into VAT.

The employee remuneration is the same. The end price is the same, and the return to the investor is the same. What has changed is that *the cost of production is now lower.*

1. The exercise highlights the amount of hidden tax in the price of the goods and services. The hidden taxes that are paid in the price are now exposed.

2. It reveals that we do not pay our tax as PAYE but that we pay all the taxes out of our net pay when we purchase goods as a consumer. Nothing can change this.

3. It highlights that British-made goods carry more tax than imported goods and explains why Britain cannot compete in the marketplace and also imported goods should carry a higher level of VAT/tax to even things up.

4. Very importantly, it reveals that the consumer is the major taxpayer. This has to be logical because the business sector is there to provide goods and services to the consumers, and whilst the business sector may actually pay most of the taxes to the government, they will always pass on the costs in the price. The rich earners are not the major taxpayers, as they will usually earn their income through businesses that pass the expense on to the consumers.

5. It has not always been clear who in the end pays the taxes. My father many years ago pointed out an article in the newspaper that, as far as I can recollect, reported that it would cost British Rail about £90,000 to give the CEO an increase of £5,000 because income tax was in the region of 90 per cent. It meant little to me then, but what it did not say was that the £90,000 would be passed on to the travelling public.

6. When we extend the removal of taxes into government operations, we will find that the cost of government will be reduced by as much as 20 per cent and the cost of all its inputs will go down because production costs in the business sector have been reduced. Here, we can include the cost of health and education, which would also be considerably reduced.

7. The tax on imported products will go up because of the increase in VAT taxes, which is only fair and reasonable and opens the market to local producers. But with the spread of taxes to the imported sector and the reduction in cost of the government, it may well be found that the actual level of VAT needed to fund a government that will cost less will be lower than expected.

8. It should now be appreciated that the majority of purchases and tax collected comes from the lower-paid workers of society, who mostly spend all their income, and that by raising their income, a relatively small amount will significantly increase the amount of tax received. It is possible to create a boom as well as a recession. Remember that more tax is collected in boom years than during a recession.

Other Taxes

Import Taxes and Duties

Where these taxes and duties are charged in connection with finished product imports or inputs into manufacturing processes, either on capital goods or raw materials, then the cost just adds to the cost of manufacture *and the price the consumer will eventually pay for the product.*

Vehicle Licences and Road Taxes

These taxes add to the cost of business inputs and more so to the distribution of products *and the price that the consumer will pay.*

The same taxes add to the cost of public and private transport, which, in turn, may result in demands for wage increases (cost of labour) and *again the price of goods and services to the consumer.*

In regard to the private motorist, *he is the end consumer, and* any increase will reduce his spending power.

It must be noted that taxes on fuels will affect the transport costs across the board and business will recover the cost from the consumer, and the consumer as the travelling public will also have to pay again.

Local Rates and Taxes

These are taxes levied on land and buildings, often rated on their position and category and payable by business and people alike. They are taxes in the same way that central government has taxes and are often controlled by the central government. It is one of the clearest examples of how central governments disguise taxation and the full extent of taxation raised giving either more subsidies or less subsidies and forcing the local authority to increase taxes when necessary.

The people usually work for business, and these taxes are paid from income earned by them. It would not matter if the company paid all these taxes on behalf of the employees and reduced their net incomes. It does make a difference from the overall position because these taxes too then become a part of the employment tax. The taxes that are paid by businesses are automatically added to the costs of the business *and add to the price that the consumer will pay.* If the individual pays, it will reduce his spending power.

Toll Gates—Fees

A new innovation! These are taxes raised to pay for access to some roads. They are expensive to collect and will add to business costs and consumer prices or will reduce consumer spending, meaning that the employer may have to pay more.

Company Taxes

These taxes are like income tax and calculated in relation to the earnings of the business and have been considered an appropriation of profits. Nevertheless, it must be taken into account as a cost prior to the return to shareholders in the overall operations of the *business and the prices charged for goods and services, which are eventually paid by the consumer.*

Tax on Interest: Tax on Dividends

This tax adds to the cost of money. Although it is deducted from the recipient, it is a cost taken into account when the investor decides to invest. The interest on the lending of that money is, therefore, that much more, and as it is either the government or the business that borrows the largest amounts, the cost will appear in the cost of production or taxes. *The consumer will eventually pay.*

VAT and Sales Tax

These taxes are added to the selling price of goods and services. VAT is added at all levels and effectively ensures that no tax is paid by business and all the tax is passed on to the end consumer. General sales tax should operate the same way but can be manipulated to leave considerable amounts of tax within the business sector, which that sector absorbs and *then recovers in the price to the consumer. The VAT and sales tax are aimed specifically at the end consumer:* It is a much easier and less costly tax to collect.

General

It must be realised by now that all taxes are, in fact, paid by the consumer, no matter what they are called or how they are applied. There are odd exceptions like inheritance tax. Most taxes will be paid by the business sector but recovered from the consumers in the price of the end products. It does not matter how the minister of finance allocates taxes; the consumer will end up paying. It is the ability of the consumer to fund all the taxes that is the final criteria.

Tax changes generally result in inflation. A single VAT system avoids this hidden inflationary effect of tax changes.

The business sector physically pays most of the taxes but does not actually bear the cost; the cost is charged to the end consumer. Business is just a funnel from the consumer to the government.

It also follows that the greater the local content of locally manufactured goods or services, the higher the tax content will be. All the input costs, which go into producing and selling the final product, contain a significant amount of the absorbed taxes. This includes all overheads as well as raw materials and packaging. The legal fees, audit fees, stationery, electricity, and water all contain these same tax elements.

These taxes, I would consider, comprise 20-30 per cent or more of the price of locally produced products and services on offer to the consumer,

If all these taxes were consolidated into VAT, the operating costs of all 'business would drop.' Better still, the operating cost of government would fall appreciably, and the rate of VAT would consequently not be as great as one might think.

It is only by going down this route that countries will be able to compete in their own and international markets. Many European countries find that they cannot compete because their cost of labour is high. They need to concentrate on lowering the cost of employment whilst increasing the spending power of the people employed.

The improved control over the economy with a single VAT system is very considerable. The economy becomes dynamic and extremely responsive to change. The conversion ratio of employee cost to spending power once it reaches close to 100 per cent means that pay increments and general inflation can be kept at a very low rate.

The British would not have lost a large part of their manufacturing industry if it had been realised that local production was carrying far more of the tax burden than imported products. Taxation made British industry uncompetitive far more than the trades unions or business managers who were blamed.

Many countries have lost their capital investment base through income taxes both on individuals and business, and vast amounts of money have ended up in offshore banks. Do away with these taxes, and this investment base would return.

Countries that opt to keep income tax, taxes on people, and the other absorbed taxes may well find that they need to keep import tariffs and export incentives to maintain their balance of payments position.

One of the objectives in the change is to ensure that imported goods and services share the same tax burden as the locally produced product. This, in turn, ensures that the government does not lose with any change in the balance of imports and local products.

Without these taxes, the cost of labour is very much less, and when the conversion factor to spending power becomes 100 per cent, employers will appreciate the benefit of rewarding employees.

A Note on VAT

The VAT system of tax can be fairly, tightly controlled and is fair in application, in which tax is paid in proportion to spending, which is usually related to earnings. Whilst the tax is paid on inputs, the tax so paid is deducted from the tax received and remittable on outputs so that no tax accrues in the production and distribution processes. It is the end consumer who pays the tax, which is, in fact, no different from the present position, except that the tax is patently obvious. The tax can be graduated so that fruits and vegetables may be 5 per cent, whilst luxuries may be 25 per cent.

Under this system, business will find it more beneficial to add to the payments of the lower-paid workers than the higher paid because the improvement in their own revenue will be better.

The tax objective changes to ensure that business does not absorb tax in order to hold down inflation and make business competitive—quite different from the tax objectives of today, which is purely to ensure that tax is paid by all means possible.

CHAPTER 6

Inflation

Inflation can be controlled, but the present accepted method of the central bank controlling the economy and inflation through interest rates is poor policy.

Inflation is the depreciating value of money represented by the rising price of goods and services to the consumer. It can be controlled. There are different ways in which this increase in price can arise.

Wage Increases

Wages traditionally increase each year, and inflation will move with the increase in wages. However, having taken income tax out of the system, wage increases would be lower.

Excessive Demand

The demand for goods and services exceeds the supply. This occurs when the spending power in the community is greater than production. It is very rarely the case in this day and age, although there was a time when credit sales were new and growing when this could have occurred, and the advocates of using interest rates to control inflation must have been around at this time. The objective of increasing interest rates was to curb the demand for goods purchased on credit and the ability of business to grant that credit. Credit has since become a way of life, and in times of high inflation, people will buy on credit as a hedge against inflation. If nothing else, demand will be satisfied through imports.

Higher Costs

Higher costs can arise through the normal conditions of supply and demand. There are various factors such as agricultural crop failures, strikes, and labour unrest at the source of supply and so on. This type of inflation will often relate to certain products and will not be the 'across the board' inflation resulting from tax increases.

However, the government controls the major source of price increases in the manner in which it runs the economy. There are two major factors interest rates and taxation.

Taxes

The fact that *all* taxes are payable by the consumer shows that any tax increases will lead to increased prices of goods and services to the consumer.

Tax increases add to the cost of production sooner or later, either directly or indirectly, through wage claims, as we have seen, and the more production processes involved or the longer the chain to the consumer, the higher the incidence of the tax change will be.

Tax changes can produce an immediate impact, or the full impact may only materialise over a period of time. Companies will sometimes opt to absorb tax increases for a time before passing the cost on to customers. Increased income tax is initially absorbed by the employee with a decrease in his spending power, which, in turn, reduces business turnover.

Imported Inflation

There is imported inflation, and there is little that can be done about it if the currency is stable and the price increases are emanating from sources beyond the control of the government. Generally, the normal laws of economics sort out the problem with innovation, substitution, or alternative suppliers or sources of supply. The effect will be on specific product areas and not general increases.

Inflationary Effects of Interest Rates

Interest rates have a direct effect on many costs of production, let alone the actual cost of borrowing money.

Returns on investments are aligned to interest rates so that the property owner looks for higher rents when interest rates escalate; the investor looks for better returns on his capital when interest rates increase so the entrepreneur has to improve his profit margins as well as meet higher rents and interest charges. Employees will have to meet higher rents or interest charges on their accommodation and will look for higher wages.

The cost of government will rise with higher interest rates because governments are amongst the largest borrowers of money, and this may lead to an increase in taxation.

As production costs increase in one industry, they will increase in another so that increasing costs will be passed from one industry to another, that is, packaging and stationery price increases distribution costs and all general expenses. All add to the final cost to the consumer.

It is not unusual to find that the government, having increased taxes and created a round of inflation, then through the central bank increases interest rates to combat the inflation. This results in a further round of inflation and higher interest rates with higher costs to government; this will require the collection of more tax, which creates a further round of inflation, requiring a further increase in interest and added inflation.

This situation can be better illustrated by stating that the government in increasing taxation has most likely reduced spending power and increased prices at the same time. There is no point in adding a further measure of increased interest rates. It is for this reason that the central bank should not be involved in the economy. The central bank can often cut off growth. The ministry of finance can control the economy through taxation far better than the bank can exercise control through interest rates.

These increases in taxation and interest rates and the inflation involved reduce spending power in the economy and can lead the way into recession. Recession itself reduces the income to government and adds to the cost of unemployment, resulting in a need for government to lift taxes higher.

In general terms, under stable conditions, the cost of products should not increase, except for wage increments. And if taxes are removed from business, including personal taxes, then costs and prices could go down with productivity going up. Inflation will be minimal.

Interest rates can be used to curb spending power in the short term only because in the longer term, it will create more inflation.

It is necessary to appreciate that people who make money from money and the money market prefer a volatile market with interest rates moving up and down; this moves property and capital gains up.

The best explanation of this is that when interest rates move upward, there is a pressure on rents and profits to move upward. When interest rates move down, rents and profits do not reduce, but the capital value of the property or investment goes up to reflect the better returns. The movement of interest creates capital gains.

CHAPTER 7

Running a Country

In this part, we will look at running a highly competitive country with maximum efficiency, the ability to achieve full employment, a stable currency, a stable economy, and the lowest level of inflation.

In the End, This Is the Only Way to Go.

Visualise the following:

A system of government in which the people in the community will enjoy the following:

- free health for the family;
- free education for the children;
- a good standard of living;
- no fears of recession;
- a low rate of inflation;
- an adequate pension at the end of the day;
- no personal taxes.

What more could they ask for?

In addition, the investors and the business sector will get the following:

- the ability to produce products at the lowest ever cost, allowing them to compete in the local and the overseas markets;
- a strong market base;
- no fear of recession;
- strong incentives to invest with no direct taxation.

Does this sound like Utopia? Is it possible to achieve all of this for sound economic reasons and not for social and political reasons?

Yes

We have seen how it is possible to make business competitive both locally and internationally and how the tax changes make a huge difference in competitiveness. The VAT charges are now spread to include imported items as well, and this tax will be contributing to the social service benefits of health, education, and pensions.

In the Interests of Keeping the Cost of Employment Down

It is necessary to keep the expenses of the people as low as possible, which is why we have free health, education, and pensions. This is why TV licences would need to go and council taxes would need to go. Council taxes would be recovered in the rate of VAT. The business sector has already been covered, and it is the individual side that would need to be covered from the additional VAT receipts and savings in government expense, which would include considerable savings in unemployment.

The revised tax system would ensure that business would expand and the realisation by employers that their sales depend on maintaining a reasonable standard of living for their employees.

Prime government policy should be to maximise employment and raise the standard of living of all with a stable currency and minimal inflation.

This can be achieved within a monetary system through a single VAT system of taxation and a minimum wage to control spending power in the economy.

There could still be excise duty in the form of social taxes on tobacco and alcohol to keep imports and consumption down. The electric motor car would also assist in keeping fuel imports down.

In the average community, there will be a relatively small number of wealthy people and a large number of average—and poor-income people. The wealthy will spend proportionately more but will not be affected by changes in minimum wages or, very often, minor tax changes. The average person will spend more as his income goes up, but his purchases will be fewer if the price or level of tax goes up. The average person has the bulk of the spending power in the economy and affects the marketplace most.

To achieve growth, we increase spending power by increasing the minimum wage or reducing the level of taxation. This increases the demand for goods and the need for workers to produce or to widen the scope for additional goods and services, which will improve employment opportunities.

Whilst it may look as if the increased spending power will create inflation, which uncontrolled it could, controlled it creates employment. *It is the most effective way to create employment.*

Business and employment can only grow and develop in good times, although there are a few businesses that will thrive during recession.

By removing the other tax elements such as income tax, a finer control over the economy can be achieved. The environment is also very attractive for investment.

Improving spending power without improving business opportunities is also somewhat of a waste because imports will flood in—a valid reason to reduce and not increase interest rates. The need to encourage investment is greater than the need to curb purchasing imports. Local investment will eventually curtail imports.

By holding down interest rates, this position tends to take care of itself because the increase in imports will affect the balance of payments, pushing the currency value down, which makes imports more expensive and local manufacturers even more attractive.

Local manufacturers require low labour and operating costs, which are achieved through low interest rates and low taxation, combined with an attractive market. A lower labour cost can be achieved in different ways as shown below:

It is necessary to maintain a ratio between production and consumer spending. If increases in spending power exceed the limit to which production can expand, then inflation will set in. The limit on growth is the ability to expand and develop productive resources. It is very dependent on the availability of skills.

If production and consumer spending is in balance, then imports and exports will balance.

If there is no income tax—all other things being equal—capital investment will be fairly, readily available. If the marketplace is solid, then private business enterprise will develop; business requires only a marketplace and people.

Of note, when there is no income tax, the incentive to 'fiddle' taxes is negligible and the collection of taxes considerably improved. The penalties for tax evasion would need to be severe.

To curb spending, power taxes should be increased, whether the government needs funds or not. It is necessary for government and the business sector to liaise on the level of payments to people. When business is doing well, it cannot reward people out of proportion because that would upset the balance, and the government would need to take up the additional spending through taxes. For this purpose only, a small amount of personal tax may be introduced, not for the purpose of providing a revenue base but for the sole purpose of economic control.

With only VAT as a tax, business enterprises have a low cost structure and so does government. Business can compete in the marketplace, both local and foreign, and the government's requirement for tax can be maintained at a low level.

It must be noted that the best deal for everyone is coming out of the changes suggested. The people of the community benefit, and the investors benefit. One has to appreciate that taxing the wealthy becomes difficult with many ways to avoid tax, and the wealthy can afford the best advice in this regard. In many, if not most, cases, the tax increases on the wealthy will end up in additional costs on products and services, and the consumer will end up paying. It is also vital to keep the wealthy in the country. It would be an economic disaster to have them leave the country because taxes were too high. The country needs them to invest in business enterprises.

With the removal of these taxes, government employees will cost less, and many of the government inputs will cost less. The cost of collecting the taxes will be less and the level of income required by the government will be that much less so that the actual amount of tax required to sustain everything will be less. Take away a large part of the cost of unemployment, and the savings are very much more.

Pensions

There is absolutely no need for fixed dates on pensions such as sixty or sixty-five, and people should work through whilst they are fit and well and able to do so, provided always that there is work available. There are many executives still working at seventy. It is good for the brain and the general well-being of the person. One may not want to work if one hates the job he or she is in, but the system intends to ensure that work is generally available and people are not stuck in jobs that they dislike. However, it has to be recognised that some people are fit, well, and capable at eighty, whilst others become incapacitated much earlier. People are living longer. People would be able to get a state pension when they retire, and it could be higher as people get older. The funding for the pensions would come from the VAT shared between imported and local goods and services.

It would become necessary to create a fund for these pensions, and it would become an ideal source from which the government could borrow.

From an Employer's Point of View

The environment created encourages investment in business and competition. The employer needs a reliable workforce with strong effective and innovative managers. It will be better able to attract these managers and experts with the absence of taxes. The marketplace will be reliable and strong with operating costs at their lowest level. Government will be working to maintain these conditions.

There will no longer be a need for investors to find tax havens from which to operate. Profit levels can be lower, whilst dividends can be maintained. Investment in business should provide better returns than investment in institutions like banks.

Businessmen and public alike may come to appreciate that they need to support local industry to ensure that their own markets remain strong and people are employed.

From a Government's Point of View

The priority of a government will be to encourage the development of industry and business and the employment of people generally. The economy will depend on people being employed at a reasonably good wage to sustain spending power in the economy. It should be unnecessary to have unemployed people, and unemployment benefits should be minimal.

The government will have a very dynamic economy, which will respond very quickly to changes. It is unlike income tax, where an adjustment will first hit spending power and then, over a period, hit prices and inflation and wage increments. A change in the rate of VAT will immediately be felt. Any such change should be done with a view to increasing or decreasing spending power in the economy. A relatively small reduction in VAT could result in more spending and effectively not change government income. An increase in VAT would reduce spending power and government income, provided the employers did not compensate the workers. However, an increase in wages would increase spending and government incomes.

The government would need to provide for normal expenses together with health and education and additionally old age pensions. The latter should be funded and investments made in such things as housing and loans for infrastructure development.

It would be vital for government to maintain competitiveness in industry and maintain an acceptable level of taxation compared to other countries.

Governments should be able to move away from incurring vast amounts of debt. They should not borrow for recurrent expenditure. Any such borrowing would indicate that it is not collecting sufficient tax.

A considerable amount of business has been lost in the United Kingdom, the United States, and Europe to countries like China and India because they were not competitive. Business may still find that Asian countries can undercut them on wages, but they have to maintain employment levels to maintain their domestic market. It is equally vital that the Asian countries pay their workers better in order to develop their own internal economies. They must not rely upon the more affluent Western economies to sustain their industries. The Asian countries must develop their own internal markets, and they should not rely on their external markets to sustain them into the future.

Free Market Competition and Other Taxes

The system lends itself to free market competition. There will always be a need to import things, particularly raw materials that are not readily available, but each country should endeavour to produce its own requirements as far as possible. It will be found that some import duties may be necessary as some industries start up, but import duties should not be a matter of course. However, VAT may well start with the importation of goods. Charging import duties on imports from cheap labour countries such as China would be acceptable in an effort to raise wages in those countries in an endeavour to improve the economies of those countries. As the wages go up so the duties come down. Businessmen taking advantage of these cheap labour markets should expect import duties and need to pay more in order to improve the purchasing power in those markets. It is not acceptable practice to manufacture goods in a cheap market to sell in a market where wages are higher and demand therefore stronger. Businessmen need to learn how to look after their markets.

Some governments may feel that they should levy taxes on what may be termed excess income or earnings; some may well be justified, but it is well to remember that the very rich are well able to manipulate things so that their income is not reduced by taxation. It is very necessary to encourage investors within the country and avoid the emigration of such people or companies to tax havens. When this system is introduced, it may well be a time for a temporary excess profits tax as many companies will see an opportunity to increase profits, which would not be the reason for changing taxes. The object is to change the tax system with a view to reducing costs and prices, and business should recognise this and reduce prices to the point where they would make the same net profit after tax as before. Government could then be justified, charging a high excess profits tax.

I would not expect the new rate of VAT to be more than 25 per cent, but I could be wrong. However, one should bear in mind that the cost of governments around the world would become comparative as and when they change.

Governments have thought up different ways and reasons for raising taxes, often without consideration of the cost of collection. It is far less expensive to collect VAT than income tax; it is much cheaper to collect road taxes through a fuel levy than through toll gates. Estate duties/death duties pose a problem because the benefactor may well ensure he accumulates more to obviate the tax or move his wealth elsewhere. The beneficiaries may well spend their new gains, creating more taxes through the VAT system. These are taxes that need to be given separate consideration, but always there is the question of investment funds and where they are located and why. Governments should take into consideration, when looking at any tax, the impact on costs and prices and the cost of collection. There is absolutely no reason why a tax should be introduced just to keep people employed.

The Effects of Taxes

Governments constantly dream up ways to increase income from different means of taxation and do not consider all the economic impacts. I have already explained how consumers are the biggest contributors one way or another. The expense of collecting the taxes must always be of vital consideration. Collecting individual income tax is far more expensive than collecting VAT. Road tolls are also expensive to collect and will increase the prices of transport and goods and services and add a little to the price of fuel, and the cost of collection is vastly reduced.

One very good example was the Poll tax in Britain—a fixed tax imposed on individuals and relatively expensive to collect, which hit the younger persons in the community including the unemployed, who spent 100 per cent of their income, with the result that sales were down and jobs were badly affected. It is vital to keep sales and the economy running, and to do that, we have to keep the community working. There was a recession, and that situation changed when the tax was removed.

Austerity

Austerity measures should never be necessary. However, they have been used where governments have over borrowed for one reason or another.

Increasing taxes, as we have seen, will have detrimental effects on the economy one way or another. It will end up in higher prices and reducing sales and employment.

Cutting down on jobs in government creates more unemployment and uncertainty and affects sales. At all times, one would expect government to ensure that its employees are efficient and effective, and it should not be possible to make large cuts in staffing levels—in particular, police, hospital staff, and education. If the people who are discharged cannot find work, then they will be needing unemployment benefits.

These are all measures that will push the country towards recession whereas extra taxes come from boom times. It may be that the currency has to be devalued to create conditions that will improve employment and remove that expense from government whilst, at the same time, pushing up sales, which will provide more tax.

CHAPTER 8

Ministry of Business

It has been recommended that we do not have income tax on companies as well as individuals. It is still necessary to have a discipline for businesses to complete annual accounts. For a number of reasons, then, I would suggest a ministry for business.

This ministry could hold, say, a small percentage, possibly 2 per cent to 5 per cent of shares in all companies and would receive annual returns and reports to ensure that the business sector is healthy. As companies are registered, they would include a 2 to 5 per cent interest for the government. In its turn, the government would ensure that the business has a sound financial base and provide assistance or guarantees for business to obtain the necessary finance for them to operate and become successful.

Interest rates are high when risks are high, and new business ventures are often in the high-risk category and may incur higher expenses than the norm. In any event, it is necessary for the government to keep interest rates at acceptable levels.

The objective of this ministry would be to keep business costs down, know where and what the country's competition is, and ensure that there is adequate employment and that the country can compete. It could become a reference point for commerce and industry and be supplementary or part of the Ministry of Trade.

It is possible that the government may need to go into business in order to create jobs in industries where entrepreneurs are not readily forthcoming. It also may do this in order to create competition where excess profits are being made.

One can consider that some hospitals and schools could become privately owned entities with the government providing an amount for each pupil to attend school. Hospitals may be awarded rates for each patient. The object of this sort of exercise is that when an individual or group of individuals has a vested interest in an enterprise, they ensure that the business is properly administered and in the best interests of their marketplace.

CHAPTER 9

What Could Happen If We Do Not Change?

The penalty for staying with the present tax systems is that countries such as Britain and America could find that they become uncompetitive in the marketplace and businesses will close or be taken over by external companies, which would possibly be Chinese. Maybe some twenty to fifty years from now, the Asian markets will have grown and the external interests may well decide to close their businesses in Britain and America as unnecessary, creating mass unemployment in those countries.

Should my advice be ignored and countries continue with the same policies into the future, then countries like Britain and America could be faced with major economic problems and huge poverty.

Taking Britain as an example, there are companies that have already moved their administration and other services to countries like India. Many major companies are foreign owned. As unemployment grows, so will taxation and so will the cost of labour. The country has already reached a point where many manufacturing companies have closed. The politicians are fighting with the finance sector, which seems to be the backbone of the economy, over payments to staff. Much of the profits of these institutions are generated outside the country, and it is possible that they may decide to move their operations to other countries.

The government may feel that they could prevent closures with a take over, but they could well find that they do not have the money and manufacturing money is another recipe for disaster.

At some time in the future, the British labour force that remains could be used to not working or not having the right work ethic. A lot of the expertise to run businesses may have been lost or died off.

At the same time, countries like China and India will have woken up, and as their workers get paid more and their internal economy grows, their reliance on exports gets less. They may well have invested heavily into Britain, Europe, and America and gained a lot of expertise. Then as their internal economy grows and the Western countries' demands for their goods wane, they may decide to close their factories and other businesses in the West, leaving a lot of unemployment.

As unemployment grows, taxation will need to rise, and the overall spending power in the country will decrease. Poverty will grow, and more businesses will close with unemployment increasing. It will be extremely difficult to stop.

Now bear in mind that the Eastern countries could plan the downfall of the Western countries economically, should they so wish. Take China with the same average wage as America has now, and it would have a bigger and stronger economy. I seem to remember a book written many years ago called *The Creed of the Third Millennium*, which starts following the economic collapse of America.

It can happen, and it is far better to ensure that it does not happen right now. It is vital to put countries on to a competitive footing and ensure that the community is employed.

CHAPTER 10

Trade and Balance of Payments

We know that countries in general should balance their books—should balance imports and exports. But many countries seem to have moved away from this discipline. There may often be some confusion with financial movements and capital purchases. It gets even more confused with the number of banks and companies able to do international transactions. There are also numerous companies and people including banks who are gambling on rates of exchange.

It is recommended that the World Bank be able to monitor these transactions. There should be a recognised world currency—on paper, that is, not in cash notes—so that all international transactions can go through that currency, and all local currencies can be quoted in a single rate to the World Bank currency. This would get rid of the need for many currency conversions and hopefully stop a lot of gambling on rates of exchange. The World Bank should be in a position to advise on exchange rates and be able to advise on where to obtain imports and where to sell exports to the best advantage of importer and exporter. There will be a need to get rid of the many exchange rates and all the different balances owed to and from different countries and enable them to be consolidated. It is essential to recognise that if countries are to retain their independence, it is essential that they do not become a constant net importer or a constant net exporter; otherwise, some countries may end up buying other countries, maybe unintentionally, but in the longer term, it could happen intentionally.

CHAPTER 11

Comment on the World at Large

One has to appreciate that Asia—mainly India and China—operates on cheap labour, and they are becoming the main manufacturing centres of the world because even Western countries are taking advantage and moving production into China. They are reliant on Western countries for their sales and export earnings to sustain their economies. As unemployment grows in the West and taxes become higher to sustain that unemployment and consumer markets shrink, Asia will need to improve their wage structures and increase their domestic markets. In this way, Asia could become one of the biggest economic entities, and Western countries would be shrinking in the absence of any sustainable development.

The Western countries have an added problem of increasing population size due to immigration—much of which is coming from Africa and the poorer countries of the world. Many people have left the African continent because of poor governance resulting in much poverty, conflict, and uncertainty. Many of the countries have suffered because of dictatorships and a lack of knowledge and experience. It is vital that these countries get on to a better political footing and be in a position to develop their economies in a peaceful fashion so that their peoples will be attracted back to their countries of origin. After all, many of these countries have rich natural resources and are capable of sustained growth.

Most of Africa is a problem to the rest of the world, and a lot of concentration and effort may be needed to improve the situation. It will require political change, and giving money and subsidies to help the starving poor may not be the right answer. People are starving to death because their leaders are unable to get things right, and many are lining their pockets instead of developing their economies for the benefit of the people. There has been, and continues to be, considerable emigration from these countries and considerable movement of people to neighbouring countries because of wars and unrest.

It is essential that countries develop decent economies, providing their communities with a reasonable standard of living. It can be done, but there is still a huge lack of understanding of politics, know-how, and leadership. There also seems to be a growing amount of corruption in governments, which needs to be stamped out.

The Euro/EEC

There was always going to be a problem with a single currency in the European Union because different countries within the EU have different political and economic policies, and as is happening, there are, and are going to be, continuing problems holding a stable EU currency.

To be successful, the EU countries would need to set up systems much the same way as in the United States of America, where there is an element of control over the economic policies at least of the various components. It is extremely difficult to operate all these different countries with one currency when one of the controls of international trade is the ability to revalue or devalue the currency. The same criteria must apply to the employment and remuneration of the individual communities, pension benefits, prices, and taxes. The work ethics of the people need to be much the same; otherwise, countries with energetic, dedicated workers would end up being in a far better position and even subsidising other countries where the work ethics are lower. There have to be government-borrowing limits laid down. A single World Bank currency would be of great assistance in the event that one of the countries would want to have its own currency so that it would have more flexibility in its monetary affairs. However, it will be found that the best option is for countries to model themselves on the most successful components. The present economic problems within the EU are solvable with the parameters above. Cure the unemployment problems by whatever means possible. Those countries with a high dependency for tourism may need the others countries to improve first.

It is difficult to see how countries can maintain their independence and be part of something like the EU without following the same rules and regulations within reason.

CHAPTER 12

Politics

Socialism and Communism

Karl Marx developed a theory to do without money so that capitalists could not accumulate wealth and exist. He envisaged the government owning and running everything and giving guidance; he did not take into consideration the human element, their abilities, and lack of their need for integrity and consideration for the community. He did not realise that money gives the people freedom, particularly freedom of choice. His system envisaged that people should work to provide themselves as the community with goods and services, basic dress with brown or black boots, without recognising that the people preferred to make a choice in what they wanted. One would end up with a regimented society with little purpose in life. Only a monetary system can provide that choice, but it also requires the innovation and production risks to provide a choice that is not part of the communist doctrine. Marxism, in its pure form, has never been tried or tested and would be found impractical. It requires a dictatorship with long-serving government officials rather than relatively short-term democratically elected leaders. This inevitably leads to dictatorships and abuse of power and corruption.

Socialism is much the same thing, where governments aim to own everything and operate all the businesses. Ministers are expected to be able to provide goods and services to the community, and again they do not appreciate the need for freedom of choice. They will ensure jobs without recognising the need for efficiency. Elected politicians do not generally have the necessary ability and drive to run businesses. When they make mistakes, they are usually big mistakes, and the people have to pay dearly. They have an entirely different viewpoint to the entrepreneur who is risking his own money in his endeavours. Dictatorships and one party states can and do arise through Communism and Socialism, where governments dictate their policies to the people. Government ministries are not really run efficiently, and government-owned businesses are run the same way. They do not know how to compete, and competition is not a part of their objectives. The system will work better where countries are reasonably self-sufficient, and they do not have to compete with other countries in the world for trade.

Why would we not want a dictator? Look at history. The olden-day kings of England and Europe were dictators, and the people were poor and suffered. All have been eradicated or their powers drastically reduced. There was Adolf Hitler, and very many more examples across the world generally were bad and responsible for genocides, mass murders, and poor governance. Russia exchanged a Tsar for a dictator, and many people perished.

Capitalism

Capitalism on the other hand provides freedom of choice with a monetary system but will put priorities around power and wealth. There is often little to stop the exploitation of the workers, and workers start trade unions for their protection. The business side will be very competitive and look to producing goods and services at the cheapest price to sell to best advantage. They do not always concern themselves with the development of the markets, and it is this area that needs to be addressed. They are not concerned with how many people are employed or not employed or where they might be employed. The government will encourage business in their endeavours to make profits in order to improve their tax income. Governments will look after business interests because they are considered to be the largest contributors to the government purse. Because of the free enterprise system, the country can have short-term democratic elections to elect government representatives.

The Centre Line (The author's Invention)

The above outlined takes a middle road and recognises that individual entrepreneurs are best suited to run businesses but entrepreneurs should begin to appreciate the role of the worker as the consumer, providing the marketplace for the goods and services produced. It recognises that the people of the community require as much freedom as possible and access to the goods and services on offer. Government income will come from the community as they spend, and the community will need to be able to earn the money to spend.

As for government, it would be recommended that there be a non-political ceremonial head or committee responsible only for dissolving parliament and calling for elections when necessary and within reasonable limits. (Britain has a queen.) This is to avoid a leader being able to become a dictator. There would be a parliament with a prime minister responsible for running the country. Parliamentarians should be selected for their honesty, integrity, and ability, and there should be no avenues for corrupt practices.

Summary

At the end of the day, Western countries must change or lose out to a developing Eastern bloc. Huge investments have been made into Western countries by China, Japan, and Arab states that have not paid sufficient attention to their own internal economies, but if and when they do, they would become the Americas of tomorrow. These countries accumulate large trade balances, which they choose to invest in countries like America, instead of developing their own internal economies.

It should be said that Western countries have also made huge investments into Eastern countries to take advantage of cheap labour. Eastern countries develop the expertise, whilst the West loses their expertise. As the cheap labour gets more expensive, those countries' economies will develop.

The world of tomorrow should see everyone contributing work wise but with a lot more time for physical activities.

CHAPTER 13

The Possible Future of the Green Theme

There are many disadvantages with railways because of their rigidity in operation and schedules. Their advantage is the movement of quantity or bulk. Motor transport is far more flexible, but there are huge problems with pollution. People prefer personal transportation to public transportation. There is also the ever-increasing congestion on roads and accidents.

Electric cars have been developed, but they have certain limitations in covering distance. Having said that, the governments should have put a lot more effort into the development of the electric car. After all, electric vehicles have been around for many years now, particularly delivery vehicles. The major advantages are that they do not consume fuel, and there is no pollution.

A new idea—how about the development of mono rails with motor cars that will convert straight on to them? There is a facility to drive on to a frame, and the car or the vehicle can then move quickly on to the rail service, having punched in the destination and a credit card. The driver can relax whilst the vehicle speeds to its destination, no matter how far away it may be. Railway operators could also operate on a go when full type of operation for commercial passenger operations.. Even the large trucks could be catered for, provided they can be loaded and despatched in a reasonable time. I am no expert in this field, but I see a lot of scope for development.

I trust that my readers have found this of interest and can do something towards achieving what is necessary. One has to think of the generations that will follow.

Peter W. Bailey
FCIS, ACMA, CGMA
Email: pwbailey@mweb.co.zw

A cost and management accountant he is used to analysing the costs of labour, and because of his business experience, he is very aware of who is actually paying the taxes. As CEO of a conglomerate in a changing climate, he was very aware of the effects of government policy changes. He has been working on this theory for many years, and this is the latest contribution in a move to lower costs for the country as a whole so that they can compete in free market economies. He has also realised that things have to change if his grandchildren are to survive in this world.

www.ingramcontent.com/pod-product-compliance
Lightning Source LLC
Chambersburg PA
CBHW021041180526
45163CB00005B/2233